YOUR KNOWLEDGE HAS VALUE

AF149583

- We will publish your bachelor's and master's thesis, essays and papers

- Your own eBook and book - sold worldwide in all relevant shops

- Earn money with each sale

Upload your text at www.GRIN.com and publish for free

Millie Patel

The Roles of IS-IT in Transforming Enterprises

With the use of the Web, E-commerce & Mobile Applications

GRIN Publishing

Bibliographic information published by the German National Library:

The German National Library lists this publication in the National Bibliography; detailed bibliographic data are available on the Internet at http://dnb.dnb.de .

Imprint:

Copyright © 2011 GRIN Verlag GmbH
Print and binding: Books on Demand GmbH, Norderstedt Germany
ISBN: 978-3-656-13825-9

This book at GRIN:

http://www.grin.com/en/e-book/189509/the-roles-of-is-it-in-transforming-enterprises

GRIN - Your knowledge has value

Since its foundation in 1998, GRIN has specialized in publishing academic texts by students, college teachers and other academics as e-book and printed book. The website www.grin.com is an ideal platform for presenting term papers, final papers, scientific essays, dissertations and specialist books.

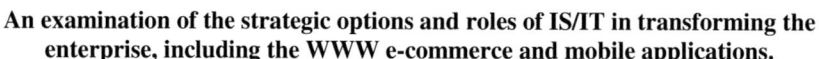

An examination of the strategic options and roles of IS/IT in transforming the enterprise, including the WWW e-commerce and mobile applications.

By: Millie Patel

Table of Contents

Title: An examination of the strategic options and roles of IS/IT in transforming the enterprise, including the WWW e-commerce and mobile applications.

Abstract

This paper focuses on the impact of Information and Communication Technologies on Enterprises and how advanced technologies are used to benefit organizations. The three main areas concerning ICT: Web 2.0, E-commerce technologies and Mobile Applications, are discussed in detail to give the readers a broader view of the potential these technologies hold for organizations all around the world. The rapid development of agile and collaborative IT infrastructures has truly changed the way of communication across different entities. Not only this, intelligent systems are being used to gather information and knowledge that can be used for greater purposes. An example of this is web analytics, to gain market intelligence on any product or service sold in any part of the world.

The Internet brings enterprises closer to their stakeholders by improving relationships. Reduced costs and increased productivity are also in the package of benefits that enterprises receive by adapting to the new environments of being, trading and communicating - online. So how do enterprises leverage the information to steer their ships to prosperity? How are enterprises gaining larger market shares and reaching wider geographical areas to spread their existence? Executives on the move are always reliant on their smart phones to stay in touch. All this, and more on the trends of technology have been looked at through this research.

This paper boils down to a literature review of lots of work done by other researchers on the same topic and compares what they say about the effects of ICT on enterprises, negative or positive.

Keywords: *Strategic Roles of ICT, Enterprises, Web 2.0, E-commerce, Mobile Applications*

Research Methodologies:

The goal of carrying out the research was to get information from different perspectives and see how they all relate to the subject matter. Research papers that have been referred to come from a different variety of authors: some in academics; some from organizations that actually make use of the available Internet technologies in carrying out their business duties (like Idea Couture and Frost & Sullivan); some from organizations that play a part in building these technologies (like IBM and Google), and articles from McKinsey that is an organization that carries out global surveys in these fields of work. Also taken into consideration are the viewpoints of the press and media associates (like The Economist and The Channel Insider). Mostly all the articles and research papers were searched for and found online, hence speeding up the research process – this could be another amazing effect of having access to Web 2.0 technologies?

Introduction

The rapid development and enhancement of Information Technologies is providing enterprises with improved ways of leveraging information and in return this change of events is positioning enterprises such that they can gain competitive advantages in several ways: they are able to penetrate markets more successfully over wider geographical areas; regardless of the product or service they provide, the internet and connectivity phenomenon is being used to increase their productivity, and they are able to effectively communicate with all the stakeholders in their respective industries and make good connections with suppliers and consumers (Vickery, et al., 2004; Ducker and Payne, 2010).

This paper will focus on the impact of the World Wide Web, E-commerce Technologies and Mobile Applications on organizations. How have enterprises taken advantage of the great network that connects everyone globally? How can organizations enhance their operations, or grow in size with the help of the online connections? What has been implemented with internet technologies to allow the organizations to change the way they conduct their business? What role do mobile applications play in transforming the enterprises? The answers to all these questions will really outline the strategic role of ICT and the link between ICT and the growth of enterprises.

The use of Web 2.0 technologies has greatly increased potential for organizations to prosper. A research carried out by McKinsey on Business Technology, in June 2008, showed that companies are increasingly using the new technologies to change the way they process data and carry out transactions. This has in turn changed some of their organizational structures (Bughin, Manyika, Miller, 2008).

The research carried out by McKinsey was looking at Web 2.0 technologies like wikis, blogs, social networks and mashups, which are applications that are designed in a way that they combine several Web 2.0 technologies to form a single tool. However, aside from these technologies, there are still more prospective developments that are yet to be exploited to their full use: Cloud Computing and mobile applications. E-commerce is only part of a popular bid in transforming enterprises.

The Effects of the World Wide Web on Enterprises

The rapidly growing Internet technologies are truly transforming the way enterprises operate on a large scale; and in several ways too (Tanburn and Singh, 2001). This paper will broadly illustrate how different aspects of the Internet, Web Applications and Mobile Applications are playing a major role in being an element of the business strategy in all major organizations. The trend where 'Web 2.0 technologies meet Enterprises' is referred to as '*Enterprise 2.0*' and it is seen as "ways of managing information to distributed, agile, collaborative work environments" (Wylie, 2009, p.2). Even the slightest introduction of a new technology in an enterprise will change the business process, hence transforming it with the hope of enhancing the business and making it profitable.

4

Wylie (2009) believes that Enterprise 2.0 is driven by three things: the available Web 2.0 technologies; the increasing demand for creating enterprise applications with the ability to make them socialized, and organizational cultures that are ready to adapt to new technologies to drive their businesses to a new level. Moote (2009) has exactly the same ideas as Wylie (2009), by stating that: 1) Organizations can rejuvenate their relationships with their stakeholders through social connectivity; 2) Organizations can improve on their business processes and operations by building strong collaborative environments, and 3) Organizational structures can be redesigned to achieve efficiency and improved productivity. While these two share the same idea, Tebbutt and Fichter (2005 cited in Pressley, 2006, p.7) talk about the negative impact of Web 2.0 in enterprises. According to their research, using wikis and blogs could jeopardise the business prospects of an organization if employees give out confidential information and share it online. This can definitely be a drawback, however for the sake of this research paper, we will look into the more positive side and examine what applications and web technologies can be used for the benefits of enterprises.

Web 2.0 Applications and Cloud Computing

Web 2.0 applications are designed and deployed using agile web technologies like Ruby on Rails, Joomla or Drupal and they are collaborative applications that are used to share information across a networked environment. According to a report by NEC Unified Solutions (2010), a good feature of Web 2.0 applications is that developers are able to re-use components which add rich functionality which can be used for many purposes. The applications are mainly rich and user-friendly, and users are able to connect with and share information, whilst improving their means of communication from not only computers or notebooks, but also from using mobile devices. This gives the users the added advantage of being online 'anytime' and 'anywhere'.

These technologies have spread like fire in the enterprise world and organizations are harnessing these tools for their own benefits by deploying these rich tools to meet their needs and achieving targets like reduced costs and improved efficiency within their fields of work (Chui, Miller, Roberts, 2009). So the next big question is what kind of applications have actually helped enterprises to connect, share information and be more available on a global scale? Like mentioned above, the use of social networks like Facebook and LinkedIn, Wikis and mashups like Google Maps are the most popular amongst major enterprises.

The CEO of Idea Couture in his report on *"How Social Technologies Can Transform the Future of Tomorrow's Enterprises"* has managed to break it down and observed that "Social Technologies are the new Business Logic" (Mootee, 2009, p.3). The main reason for Social Technologies to be adapted by enterprises is to gain market intelligence and to improve their communication techniques. Mootee's report claims that a certain degree of knowing the perspective of stakeholders on the organization's products and services can be really helpful in working towards improvement and being better, hence gaining competitive advantage over rival companies.

5

Another major development in enhanced technologies brings along the beginning of a fairly new era: Cloud Computing. Bughin, Chui and Manyika (2010, p.10) define cloud computing as "accessing computer resources provided through networks rather than running software or storing data on a local computer". The technology that drives cloud computing is virtualization. Cloud computing provides virtual resources as a service over the Internet and users only pay for what they use. For enterprises, it's like outsourcing the entire IT department. This is an advantage for organizations as it almost eliminates all IT costs of installing hardware and software, maintenance costs and so on (Chang, Abu-Amara, Sanford, 2010).

The Trends of E-Commerce & Its Impact on Enterprises

With developments in the Internet and Web-based technologies, there have been many differences between traditional markets and the global electronic marketplace. This gives enterprises the ability to determine emerging opportunities and utilize the necessary skills (such as intellectual resources over the Internet) to make the most of these opportunities. An example of such an opportunity which can take an enterprise to a whole new level is E-commerce: the act of carrying out business transactions over the Internet (Pearson and Grandon, 2002, p.1). As cited in the paper by Pearson and Grandon on the *Strategic Value and Adoption of Electronic Commerce,* "improvements in product quality and the creation of new ways of selling products" are benefits of this great technology.

There is a significant movement in technology in terms of the web tools that are being used today. Previously, websites were meant to be informational; just to provide details about products and services offered by an enterprise, but the trend now is to carry out transactions and money transfers over the Internet (Regan, 2002). E-commerce allows users and enterprises to carry out dealings like shopping, banking, bill payments, auctions and lots of other things online.

Not only do organizations benefit with implementing E-commerce strategies in their organizations, but this concept also has an immense impact on the consumers; the access and ability to purchase anything they want, online, with the added ease of making transactions. Jiang and Yu (2009) have studied the relationship between enterprise strategy and e-commerce and they conclude that e-commerce is not only about buying and selling products and services online, but also about increasing the efficiency of the business supply chains, as well as knowledge management of market position.

Popular examples of E-commerce websites are Amazon and E-bay, but enterprises have also set up their online presence to sell their products and services, like supermarkets, travel agencies, restaurants etc. The internet is tool of trade in almost all industries and fields of work. Not only at the enterprise level, but E-commerce technologies have spread vastly at an industry level. We can see the implementation of IT in the banking, education, healthcare and travel and tourism industries, as well (Goldmanis, *et al.,* 2009).

Zorayda Ruth (2003) in her paper also contributes to the concepts of e-commerce and helps the reader better understand the implications of such online trade. According to her, for an organization to incorporate E-commerce facilities, lots of departments can be affected with the way they carry out their business operations, such as purchase order processing, inventory management, distribution channel management and payment management.

However the invention of such technologies does not end here. E-commerce and web technologies have spread rapidly to the mobile environment. The development and smart phones and smart applications allow enterprises to broaden their reach of the markets, not only by advertising their products or services, but also by making their shopping carts available from mobile devices. This is a huge trend and in future it will definitely reap great benefits for both enterprises as well as for consumers (Tsai, Bond, Raj, 2005).

The Impact of Mobile Applications on Enterprises

The growth of mobile technology and mobile applications are in essence driven by the same factors that brought the change in the course of actions to achieve business strategies - the development of Information Technology, mainly channelled to improve business processes and operations, and all for the same goal: to achieve competitive advantage (Kevin Burden, Oct 2005). The evolution of technology in creating smart phones and smart applications has benefited organizations worldwide. The new technology brings flexibility to the business processes and this has proved to generate good returns. Mobile applications in the past have mainly been used to broadcast information, however with recent trends, applications are also being built to gather information or to optimize organizations procedures like production planning, inventory management and logistics. Kevin Burden (2005) claims that the use of enterprise applications through mobile devices has transformed processes especially by improving the decision-making processes.

The use of mobile applications has the potential of providing enterprises with the means of achieving "better productivity and efficiency", as cited in Basole's (2005, p.3) paper on "Transforming Enterprises through Mobile Applications". Mobile applications have been implemented and deployed in several industries of work and statistics show that the incorporation of this mobile technology into the organization has improved operational performance, as well as customer service. It has also given organizations a means to communicate effectively and enhanced the business processes (Gebauer & Shaw, 2004).

The new functionalities and capabilities that mobile information and communication technologies bring have not yet been fully exploited. Mobile technology is also supporting customer interactions, cost reduction and opportunities to gain increased revenues (IBM, 2009). This can be backed up by research carried out by Kalakota and Robinson (2001 cited in Tsai, Bond, Raj, 2005, p.2), when they acknowledged that the implementation of mobile solutions is a recent but growing trend with enterprises; with an aim of examining enterprise mobility. It would be safe to say that with the rapid development of these technologies, enterprises in the future will definitely be able to exploit these opportunities to work in their benefit, and use this technology to prosper in their relative fields of work.

IBM's article on "the mobile revolution" (2009, p.4) shows how mobile technologies and applications strengthens all kinds of connectivity, worldwide. Enterprises are grabbing these opportunities to stay competitive by offering services via mobile phones or smart phone applications. These services could vary from providing customer service to allowing customers to manage their finance with the use of mobile applications (particularly in the banking sector).

In Kenya, the largest mobile network operator, Safaricom, has developed a service they call 'M-PESA', which in English translates to 'Mobile Money'. M-PESA subscribers have the ability to send money (funds) from one mobile device to another or pay their utility bills directly from their phones (Safaricom, 2010).

Google, the largest multinational Cloud Computing and Internet Search Technologies Corporation is also playing a role in transforming enterprises by developing applications that can allow users to easily manage their emails, develop a marketplace, and use other collaboration software to share information (Nurik, 2010). Google Apps support many '*smart*' mobile devices today, including the BlackBerry. Apple and Microsoft have reacted by showing signs of being threatened by Google. While making a statement about Google with the press, Steve Jobs, the CEO of Apple made that clear when he said, "Make no mistake, they want to kill the iPhone" (Channel Insider, 2010).

A report by the *Economist* (2004) on the commercial impact of mobile computing, acknowledges that most organizations today are using wireless technologies to exchange information. According to the author of that article, Jones, Wireless Internet is more reliable at times and with the growing speeds from the Internet Service Providers (ISPs), it seems to be the best way enterprises can get connected.

The table below shows some of the applications used in enterprises: web or mobile

Category	Application
Communications	E-mail, Messaging, Video Conferencing, Information Management
Supply Chain Management	Inventory Management, Real-time Tracking Systems
Customer Relationship Management	Sales Management, Contact Management, Customer Information Database Management
Enterprise Resource Planning	Invoicing Systems, Order Management
Human Resources	Time and Expense Tracking
Mobile Commerce	Mobile Banking, SMS Alerts, Advertising and Marketing

Table 1. Mobile Enterprise Applications. Taken from Basole (2005)

It is clear that the new developments of online technologies, both for the Web and for Mobiles - targeted at enterprise use - are taking into consideration business processes and this has a huge impact on the way an organization makes business transactions or operates, in general. Basole (2005, p.4) also concludes that "mobile enterprise solutions have a value and impact far beyond today's applications".

The Benefits of Web 2.0, E-commerce Capabilities and Mobile Applications

The combined effects of emerging Internet technologies have increased computing power, and pervasive digital communications are spawning new ways to manage assets and operations, and this in return is changing organizational structures. The ways information technologies are deployed are changing too, as new developments such as virtualization and cloud computing reallocate technology costs and usage patterns while creating new ways for individuals to consume goods and services and for enterprises to implement viable business models (Bughin and Chui, 2010).

As firms become aware of the Internet's advantages, more and more of them join the network, eager to exploit the tools and services the Internet offers for various business aspects such as marketing, sales, and customer support. Presently, many firms are caught up in the excitement about the remarkable growth and potential of the Internet (Stobbe, 2010). The interactive nature of the Internet medium means that firms can obtain important and quick feedback that will allow them to produce higher-quality products. Organizations can offer information about their products, services, and software for trial use while users get first-hand information about the products and services from vendors directly. Advertising on the Internet does and will continue to exist in appropriate and responsible ways that benefit both vendors and customers.

By disrupting traditional business models, technology is changing rapidly in areas such as wireless communications, sensors, and social networks. New technologies could extend the reach of organizations, improve management decisions, and speed the development of new products and services. The adoption of technology is a global phenomenon, and the intensity of its usage is particularly impressive in emerging markets (Milroy, 2010).

Social Networking can also be categorized as a great mover-and-shaker in changing some aspects of business operations. This trend has lead to changes in organizational structures too (Mootee, 2009). Social technologies facilitate a new language for communication with customers and stakeholders. Mootee also suggests that social technologies can be used as a platform to reinforce an organization's purpose and mission, and it can also be used to energize and engage employees. All enterprises need to be social. It is not a solution to improve current information systems and processes, but rather a new way of connecting, competing and collaborating creatively.

Milroy (n.d.) also concludes that Web and Mobile applications offer immediate benefits to organizations in terms of management roles and logistics, improved planning and decision making, and well collaborated environments for sharing information.

What Lies in the future?

After seeing so many developments towards Web 20, Mobile Applications and Enterprise 2.0, perhaps the next big step is to move forward to a 3.0 environment. A good question would be how will Web 3.0 be different from Web 2.0? What new capabilities and functionalities does the future hold, for individuals, enterprises, and even industries?

In 2006, Markhoff of The New York Times, described the concept of Web 3.0 as the "Semantic Web", as cited in Gardner's (2009) paper on the "use of Web 2.0". The Semantic Web will be more intelligent and will have improved ways for enterprises to manage operations, streamline processes and maintain their supply chain management. It will also remove communication barriers by a great extent (Decker *et al.*, 2010).

Conclusion

Several researchers show the positive edge of rapidly developing Web and Mobile Technologies and how they benefit enterprises and organizations, on a daily basis. From the extensive research carried out, there is an understanding that technologies affect at least three spans of business organizations: B2E (Business to Employees), by internal collaboration and co-ordination to streamline processes; B2S (Business to Suppliers), by using web tools or mobile applications to improve the supply chains, and B2C (Business to Consumers), by enhancing customer service and relations through the use of Web 2.0 and mobile communication tools (IBM, 2009).

Although this is not just the only good thing enterprises get from embracing these technologies. Some research mentioned above also shows how adapting to the new Internet and Wireless era gives organizations a competitive advantage, reduces their costs and improves their productivity. Efficiency is also a key element achieved in this case.

References

Vickery, et al. (2004). ICT, E-Business and SMEs. In: OECD (Organization for Economic Co-operation and Development), *2nd OECD Conference of Ministers Responsible for SMEs.* Istanbul 3-5 June 2004. France: OECD.

Mike Ducker and Judy Payne. (2010). *Information Communication Technology as a Catalyst to Enterprise Competitiveness.* [online] Business Growth Initiative. Available from: https://www.businessgrowthinitiative.org/BGIProducts/Documents/ICT as a Catalyst Final.pdf [Accessed: 3rd December 2010]

Bughin J., Manyika J., Miller A. (2008). Building the Web 2.0 Enterprise. *McKinsey Global Survey Results,* Fall Issue, p.3.

Jim Tanburn and Alwyn Didar Singh. (2001). *ICTs and Enterprises in Developing Countries: Hype or Opportunity?* [online] International Labour Office Geneva. Available from: http://www.ilo.org/wcmsp5/groups/public/---ed_emp/---emp_ent/---ifp_seed/documents/publication/wcms_117716.pdf [Accessed: 3rd December 2010]

Steve Wylie. (2009). Enterprise 2.0: What, Why and How. *In Enterprise 2.0 Conference.* Boston, 23-25 June 2009. San Francisco: UBM TechWeb.

Idea Couture Inc. (2009). *How Social Technologies Can Transform the Future of Tomorrow's Enterprises.* San Francisco, USA: Idea Couture Inc.

Lauren Pressley. (2006). *Using Social Software for Business Communication.* [online] Lauren Pressley. Available from: http://laurenpressley.com/papers/socialsoftware_business.pdf [Accessed: 12th December 2010]

Anon. (2010). *Converging Enterprise Communications, IT and the Cloud.* [online] Cambridge, UK: NEC Unified Solutions. Available from: http://www.nec-philips.co.uk/pdf/White paper - converging enterprise communications IT and cloud FINAL.pdf [Accessed: 7th December 2010]

Chui M., Miller A., Roberts R. (2009). Six Ways to make Web 2.0 Work: Web 2.0 tools present a vast array of opportunities – for companies that know how to use them. *The McKinsey Quarterly,* Business Technology, p.1-3.

Bughin J., Chui M., Manyika J. (2010). Clouds, Big Data and Smart Assets. *The McKinsey Quarterly,* August 2010 Issue, p.10.

Chang W., Abu-Amara H., Sanford J. (2010).*Transforming Enterprise Cloud Services.* [online] California, USA. Springer. Available from: http://ebookee.org/Transforming-Enterprise-Cloud-Services_848759.html. [Accessed: 25th December 2010]

Pearson J., Grandon E. (2002). *Perceived Strategic Value and Adoption of Electronic Commerce: An Empirical Study of Small and Medium Sized Businesses.* 36th Hawaii International Conference on System Sciences. IEEE Computer Society

Regan. (2002). *Doing Business on the Internet.* [online] February 2002. Available from: http://www.osra.org/2002/regan.pdf. [Accessed: 12th December 2010]

Jiang Y., Yu S. (2009). The Empirical Study of Relationship between Enterprise Strategy and E-commerce. *2nd Symposium International Computer Science and Computational Technology.* China, 26-28 December 2009. China: Academy Publisher.

Goldmanis M. *et al.* (2009). *E-commerce and Market Structure.* [online] Chicago, USA: University of Chicago. Available from http://home.uchicago.edu/~syverson/ecommerce.pdf [Accessed: 17th December 2010]

Zorayda Ruth Andam. (2003). *E-commerce and E-business.* [online] Kuala Lumpur, Malaysia: UNDP-APDIP, e-ASEAN Task Force. Available from: http://www.apdip.net/publications/iespprimers/eprimer-ecom.pdf. [Accessed: 18th December 2010]

Tsai, Bond A., Raj G. (2005). *Mobile Business: An Exploratory Study to Define a Framework for the Transformation Process.* Unpublished.

Kevin Burden. (2005). *Business Benefits of Industry-Specific Mobile Applications.* Massachusetts, USA: IDC, (IDCUS05WP002469)

Gebauer J., Shaw M. (2004). Success Factors and Impacts of Mobile Business Applications: Results from a Mobile e-Procurement Study. *International Journal of Electronic Commerce.* 8 (3) p.19-41.

IBM. (2009). *Enterprise Mobility: Connecting to a World of Opportunity.* New York, USA: IBM, (CIW03055-USEN-00)

Safaricom. (2010). *M-PESA Services.* [online] Nairobi, Kenya: Safaricom. Available from: http://www.safaricom.co.ke/index.php?id=257 [Accessed: 20th December 2010]

Nurik L. (2010). Is Google Eyeing the Mobile Enterprise with New Management Tools? *Channel Insider.* 8th February.

Jones, T. (2004). Cutting the cord: The Commercial Impact of Mobile Computing. *Economist Intelligence Unit.* January 2004.

Basole R. (2005).Transforming Enterprises through Mobile Applications. [online] *11th Americas Conference of Information Systems.* Omaha, NE, USA 11 – 14 August 2005. Available from http://aisel.aisnet.org/cgi/viewcontent.cgi?article=1901&context=amcis2005 [Accessed: 20th December 2010]

Bughin J., Chui M. (2010). The rise of the Networked Enterprise: Web 2.0 finds its Payday. *The McKinsey Quarterly,* December 2010 Issue, p.7.

Stobbe A. (2010). *Enterprise 2.0: How Companies are Tapping into the Benefits of Web 2.0.* [online] Deutsche Bank Research September 2010. Available from http://www.slideshare.net/fred.zimny/deutsche-bank-research-how-companies-are-tapping-the-benefits-of-web-20 [Accessed: 21st December 2010]

Milroy A. (n.d.). *Mobile Enterprise Applications in Australia.* [online] Australia: Frost & Sullivan. Available from http://www.telstraenterprise.com/SiteCollectionDocuments/Whitepapers/Moblile_Apps_White_Pape r.pdf [Accessed: 21st December 2010]

Gardner J., (2009). *New Perspectives on the use of Web 2.0 by Statistical Offices.* [online] UNECE. Available from http://www.unece.org/oes/nutshell/2009/11_Stats.pdf [Accessed: 21st December 2010]

Decker *et al.*(2010). Knowledge Networking: The Semantic Web – The Roles of XML and RDF. *IEEE Internet Computing* [online] 1089-7801/00 (September - October 2010) Available from http://www.few.vu.nl/~frankh/postscript/IEEE-IC00.pdf [Accessed: 29th December 2010]